I0599931

GO TURBO

EXTREME SURVIVAL

JIM BRUSH

LONDON·SYDNEY

First published in 2009 by
Franklin Watts
338 Euston Road
London NW1 3BH

Franklin Watts Australia
Level 17/207 Kent Street
Sydney NSW 2000

Series editor: Adrian Cole
Art director: Jonathan Hair
Design: Blue Paw Design
Picture research: Sophie Hartley
Consultants: Fiona M. Collins and Philippa Hunt, Roehampton University

A CIP catalogue record for this book is available from the British Library.

ISBN: 978 0 7496 8663 5

Dewey Classification: 796.04' 6

Acknowledgements:

Blickwinkel/Alamy: 13bl & 40. Yvette Cardozo/Alamy: 34l. Rob Cousins/Alamy: 15. Extreme Sports Photo/Alamy: 20. David Forster Life/Alamy: 11tl. Geoffrey Grace/Alamy: 17t. Harwood Photography/Alamy: 10. Josh McCulloch/Alamy: 21t. Alex Segre/Alamy: 7b & 36. Benjamin Stansall/Alamy: 6. Ariadne Van Zandbergen/Alamy: 17b. © Bettmann/Corbis: 21b. © Ashley Cooper/Corbis: 41. © epa/Corbis: 32. © Anthony Bannister; Gallo Images/Corbis: 37b. © Robert Garvey/Corbis: 34-35. © Rob Howard/Corbis: 38. © Layne Kennedy/Corbis: 18-19. © Caroline Penn/Corbis: 31. © Roger Ressmeyer/Corbis: 13tr.. © David Samuel Robbins/Corbis: 12-13. © Claire Leimbach/Robert Harding World Imagery/Corbis: 14. © Joel W. Rogers/Corbis: 7. © David Spurdens/Corbis: 3 & 18t. © Oliver Strewe/Corbis: 16. © Stuart Westmorland/Corbis: 39. © iStockphoto.com/Marina Alexandrova: Cover b. © iStockphoto.com/BMPix: 30. © iStockphoto.com/bratan007: 10b. © iStockphoto.com/Roberto Caucino: Cover t. © iStockphoto.com/Neta Degany: 17l. © iStockphoto.com/Alfonso de Tomás Gargantilla: Endpapers. © iStockphoto.com/HiM: 33b. © iStockphoto.com/Dietmar Klement: 17r. © iStockphoto.com/Sandra Kourey: 11cl. © iStockphoto.com/Albert Lozano: 10tr. © iStockphoto.com/Vasko Miokovic: 10cr. © iStockphoto.com/Sabrina dei Nobili: 11br. © iStockphoto.com/pomortzeff: 7t, 35t. © iStockphoto.com/Jennifer Richards: 17cr. © iStockphoto.com/Alexey Romanov: 11cr. © iStockphoto.com/Ian Scott: 29. © iStockphoto.com/Ales Veluscek: 11tr. © iStockphoto.com/Anna Yu: 11bl. Mary Evans Picture Library: 8. Pat Wellenbach/AP/PA Photos: 28. Chris Radburn/PA Archive/PA Photos: 9. © IFC Films/Everett/Rex Features: 33t. Sipa Press/Rex Features: 37t. Adam Hart-Davis/Science Photo Library: 18b. © Shutterstock.com/Angela Creekmur: 17cl. © Shutterstock.com/Daren Horwood: 31 (inset). © Shutterstock.com/Alexey Stiop: 28-29.

Every attempt has been made to clear copyright. Should there be any
inadvertent omission please apply to the publisher for rectification.

Printed in China

Franklin Watts is a division of Hachette Children's Books,
an Hachette UK company.
www.hachette.co.uk

*Every effort has been made by the Publishers to ensure that the websites
in this book contain no inappropriate or offensive material. However,
because of the nature of the Internet, it is impossible to guarantee that the
contents of these sites will not be altered. We strongly advise that Internet
access is supervised by a responsible adult.*

Contents

Words that are highlighted can be found in the glossary.

What is extreme survival?

Extreme survival is about staying alive in the wildest places on Earth. People use special skills to survive.

These survival skills are also known as **bushcraft**. Bushcraft experts can build a shelter, create a fire or find their way without a map. They can find food or hunt animals.

Bushcraft experts light fires with a spark and **tinder**.

Every **wilderness** has its own dangers. In the rainforest, it's easy to get lost. Deserts are baking hot. In the Arctic it is freezing cold.

The Arctic

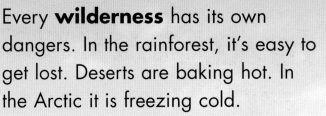

Desert

Rainforest

? Which of the three places listed above are you most interested in learning more about, and why?

Be prepared!

Explorers plan their adventures carefully. They think about where they are going and what they need to take. They follow the **Scout** motto: **"Be prepared"**.

GT Top Fact

Most explorers take only what they need. But in 1860, Robert Burke and William Wills (above centre) set off across Australia with 8 tonnes of food, a bath and a dining table. They left most of it in the desert.

Food and water are important for survival, but how much explorers need depends on where they are going. A journey across the desert needs lots of water. But polar explorers know they can boil snow on the way. What else will they need?

Will Gow and Henry Adams with their Antarctic expedition gear.

ONLINE//:

www.scouts.org.uk
Visit this website to find out more about the Scouts and the wide range of activities they organise on land, at sea – and in the air.

Essential kit

Imagine you're an explorer lost in the wild. Don't panic! A few pieces of kit can help you stay alive.

A sharp knife does lots of jobs, from cutting wood to skinning an animal.

A **compass** helps to find a direction.

Flares attract attention in an emergency.

GT Top Fact

Canadian bushcraft expert Mors Kochanski once said: "The more you know, the less you carry."

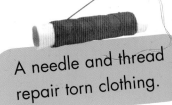
A needle and thread repair torn clothing.

A **fire steel** or matches are a quick way to start a fire.

Fishhooks and line make catching fish a lot easier.

Candles provide light at night.

Go Turbo Survival Skill

A medical kit is vital. In 1844, explorer David Livingstone was attacked by a lion in Africa. Later, he was hit in the eye by a branch. Then he nearly went deaf due to fever.

ONLINE//:

www.bushcraftuk.com
This really interesting website has some great real-life stories of people who survived in the wilderness, plus lots of downloadable factsheets.

Lost!

Many explorers can find their way with just a compass. If they don't have one, there are other ways to find their direction.

If explorers don't have a map, they make one. They climb up a nearby hill to see further. They use a compass to find north, then look for rivers and other features to use as markers.

GT Top Fact

To find north without a compass in Europe or North America, look for the Pole Star (circled). In Australia, the Southern Cross points to the south.

Go Turbo Survival Tip

Some plants can show the way. The compass plant (left) in North America has leaves that always point north–south. Or, in South Africa, north pole plants lean north.

Explorers also use the Sun to find their way. During the day, the Sun rises in the east and sets in the west. At night, stars can point the way. At sea, seaweed or seabirds can show that land is near.

ONLINE//:

www.us.orienteering.org
Website of the US Orienteering Federation, with links showing you how to use a compass, gear you'll need and an orienteering video.

Finding water

A human can survive for three weeks without food, but only three days without water. Bushcraft experts always look for more water before they run out.

GT Top Fact

In the past, **Aborigines** made long journeys across the deserts of Australia. One survival skill was to dig for desert frogs that store water in their bodies.

If there are no streams or pools, water can be found by digging in dry river beds or looking into rocky gaps. Also, plants such as bamboo, vines and some roots hold water. Rainwater can be collected in a sheet or container.

Drinking rainwater from a cut vine in the rainforest.

Experts save water by staying in the shade to avoid sweating. They also only talk when they need to. Drinking pee or salty seawater are not good ideas.

ONLINE//:

www.cultureandrecreation.gov.au/articles/indigenous/ trackers   This site by the Australian government looks at the remarkable tracking skills of the Aboriginal peoples of Australia.

Hunting and fishing

Bushcraft experts know what wild plants can be eaten. They can also track and hunt animals. Food found in the wild is sometimes called bush tucker.

Australian honey ants are rich in **nutrients** and water.

All sorts of plants can provide food – from stewed seaweed and cups of pine needle tea to bamboo shoots. But some plants are **poisonous**, so only experts should find bush tucker.

Hunters learn where an animal sleeps and eats. They catch small animals such as lizards and rabbits in simple traps, like this (right).

 Paw prints and droppings show what animals are nearby. Try to work out what made these four tracks:

A

B

C

D

Tribesmen in parts of Africa learn how to hunt as they grow up.

ONLINE//:

www.bear-tracker.com
If you fancy tracking down some animals in North America, this site is a great place to start. It includes the tracks shown above.

Fire and shelter

In the wild, building a fire provides heat and cooks food. A shelter offers protection from the Sun, wind and rain – and even wild animals.

Bushcraft experts can start a fire by creating sparks to set dry grass alight. They hit **flint** with a steel knife, use a fire steel or use a bow and drill (left). They add dry twigs and leaves, called tinder, to get the fire going. Then they put larger sticks on top.

A lightweight tent makes a great shelter. But a simple shelter can be made from a fallen tree or cut branches. A plastic sheet or bamboo poles make good shelters too.

GT Top Fact

A Native American shelter, called a **tipi**, can be put up quickly. A fire is often built inside and the steep sides keep off the rain and snow.

ONLINE//:

www.tipi.com/designyourown.html
Use this website as a starting point for designing a model tipi out of paper, complete with downloadable resources.

On the move

In the wild explorers walk at a steady pace and keep alert. It's easy to fall down a cliff, be swept away by a river, or fall into a frozen lake.

How people travel depends on where they are. Cutting through thick rainforest is hard work, so it might be easier to build a raft and float down a river. In a desert, walking at night avoids the hot Sun.

Arctic explorers use sledges to carry their gear.

Many explorers use a **scout** to find the best route. They go ahead and spot dangerous cliffs and rivers.

This man is using walking poles to help cross a fast-flowing river.

GT Top Fact

Between 1803–6, Meriwether Lewis and William Clark paddled along rivers to cross North America. On the way, waterfalls and **rapids** smashed their canoes.

ONLINE//:

www.lewisclark.net
Find out more about the explorers Lewis and Clark and their amazing expedition across North America, including journals and maps.

Rainforests

In the rainforest, it's hot and sweaty. Trekking through the forest is hard work. Jaguars, crocodiles and snakes can kill. Creepy crawlies give a painful bite.

Trekking in the Amazon rainforest in South America.

In 1971, teenager Juliane Koepcke survived a plane crash in the Amazon rainforest. The other 92 passengers died. She followed rivers downhill and walked out of the jungle 10 days later, with a torn miniskirt and one sandal.

Rainforest explorers wear boots and special wraps around the bottom of their trousers. This stops **leeches** getting on their skin (above). At night, they sleep under nets to protect against mosquitoes. A mosquito bite can give people a deadly disease called **malaria**.

ONLINE//:

http://www.exploratorium.edu/frogs/rainforest/ index.html   Audio clips of frogs in the rainforest – close your eyes and imagine what it's like to be lost.

Holiday From Hell

Written by Leon Read   Illustrated by Kevin Hopgood

The chopper span in the air, an alarm screeching, "Pull up! Pull up!" The engine made a terrible grinding noise.

Mal held on. His dad's face was calm.

"We're going down!" the pilot screamed.

The forest rushed up towards them quickly as the chopper fell.

Branches snapped, metal ripped and Mal screamed as they fell through the trees.

That was four days ago. Mal had come out to visit his dad in Brazil. Now they were lost in the Amazon forest. Mal sat near the fire his dad had made. Despite the heat, Mal pulled his jacket tighter. The mosquitoes were everywhere. Mal felt his head. He'd gashed it, but his dad had cleaned and dressed it. They had been lucky. They had buried the dead chopper pilot out in the rainforest, away from the camp.

"How's your arm?" Mal asked, swatting at the mosquitoes.

"I still can't move it. We've got to hike out of here, before it gets worse."

"You don't think anyone saw our fire?" Mal asked.

"I wish they had," Mal's dad looked up. "But the canopy is too thick. The smoke can't get through it. The radio in the chopper was smashed, and the mobile reception here is terrible."

"Some holiday this has turned out to be," Mal joked.

But Mal's dad saw the concerned look on his son's scratched face. "Don't worry," he smiled, "we'll make it."

In the morning, Mal sat looking at the wall of green forest. He hadn't really slept, there were too many noises in the forest: birds, monkeys, frogs, bugs, jaguars...

"Everything is in the backpack," his dad said, "apart from the crash axe." Mal had found it in the wreckage, along with a first-aid kit, flare gun, torch, a cigarette lighter and toffees.

He'd also found two bottles of water. They had drunk most of the water already, and filled one bottle with rainwater. It was raining again now. Heavy, thick rain that soaked right through.

Mal and his dad headed downhill. "If we follow the land down," Mal's dad said, "hopefully it will lead us to a river. We might get help from a passing boat."

Mal used a stick to move through the thick, gloomy forest. To save energy Mal's dad hacked at vines only when he needed to. They had eaten their packed lunches over the first few days. They only had fruit left, taken from the trees where they saw monkeys eating.

"So, what's the first thing you want to do back home?" Mal's dad asked, trying to keep Mal thinking about anything but the forest.

"Eat the biggest burger and fries ever!" Mal said.

They hiked all day and had one toffee and several cups of water each. They made camp before it became dark. Both of them felt weak. Tomorrow they would continue to follow the streams of water. Hoping – praying – they would lead them out of this hell.

On the third day, they were walking when Mal's dad stopped suddenly.

"Do you hear that?"

Mal listened. It sounded like water.

They walked on, a little faster. Mal's body seemed to stop aching. The trees thinned out and Mal saw water shimmering ahead.

They walked out from the trees, on to the bank of a wide river. Across the river was a village, with children playing in a clearing and boats moored along the riverbank. Mal reached into the backpack and handed a flare to his dad. They fired it into the sky together, and watched as the red, smoking flare drifted down and the children waved.

Lost at sea

The ocean is a tough place to stay alive. Storms cause high waves and the hot Sun can quickly burn skin and cause dehydration.

In 1982, Steve Callahan (below) was crossing the Atlantic Ocean. His boat sank in a storm. For the next 76 days, he survived in a tiny raft.

Steve made a spear to catch fish and seabirds. He fought off sharks that attacked his raft. When Steve's raft sprang a leak, he kept it afloat. He drifted almost 3,000 kilometres before he was spotted by a fishing boat. Later, he wrote a book: *Adrift – Seventy-six days lost at sea.*

Go Turbo Survival Skill

Steve used a solar still. This uses the heat of the Sun to turn salty seawater into drinking water.

1. Dome lets in sunlight and traps heat.

2. Heat from the Sun's rays evaporates seawater.

Solar still

3. Evaporated seawater condenses (cools and becomes water) and flows into the rim.

4. Distilled water (water separated from sea salt) collects in a container.

ONLINE//:

www.wilderness-survival.net
A great source of survival stories both at sea and on land, as well as good information on equipment and planning.

Island survivor

Some people who survive a shipwreck find themselves alone on an island. What should you do?

Follow this simple checklist:
- Check yourself for injuries.
- Look for radios, knives and other useful items that have washed up on the beach.
- Look for fresh water and build a shelter.
- Build a fire to keep warm at night. It will also be a signal for help.

A shipwreck is pounded by the waves.

Go Turbo Survival Skill

Coconuts are good to drink and eat, and their oil can protect against sunburn. Build a **SOS** signal using stones or rocks. Don't write it in sand – it will get washed away!

GT Top Fact

Scottish sailor Alexander Selkirk (1676–1721) spent four years as a castaway on a deserted island. The book *Robinson Crusoe* is based on his story.

Finding food is important for an island survivor. Climb a tree for coconuts, or hunt crabs and fish in rockpools, but watch out for sharp rocks and big waves!

ONLINE//:

www.youtube.com
If you type Ray Mears into the search box, you can track down some video clips of this bushcraft expert explaining all sorts of survival skills.

Mountains

On a mountain there is very little food or shelter. Plane crash survivors and lost mountaineers need both skill and luck.

Crash survivors can find shelter among rocks or in the plane wreckage. They can wrap themselves in blankets to keep warm. For most people, it is safer to wait until rescue comes.

Mountaineers who get lost can use ropes and other equipment to climb down. They watch out for falling rocks and **avalanches**.

GT Top Fact

In 1985, Joe Simpson broke his leg climbing in Peru. He crawled down to safety. Later, he wrote a book called *Touching The Void*, which was turned into a film (left).

Go Turbo Survival Skill

Grizzly bears live in mountain areas of North America and Canada. Most will see you as a tasty snack. What should you do if you are attacked?

ONLINE//:

www.kids.nationalgeographic.com/Animals/CreatureFeature/Brown-bear   There's a whole range of facts, photos and video clips on brown bears at this site.

Deserts

Deserts are beautiful but deadly places. In a hot desert, a person without the right clothes, water and shade in the morning could be dead by evening.

Light clothes and wide hats help people to keep cool. However, at night deserts get very cold, so warm clothes are also needed. Tough boots protect feet against sharp cactus spines and snakes.

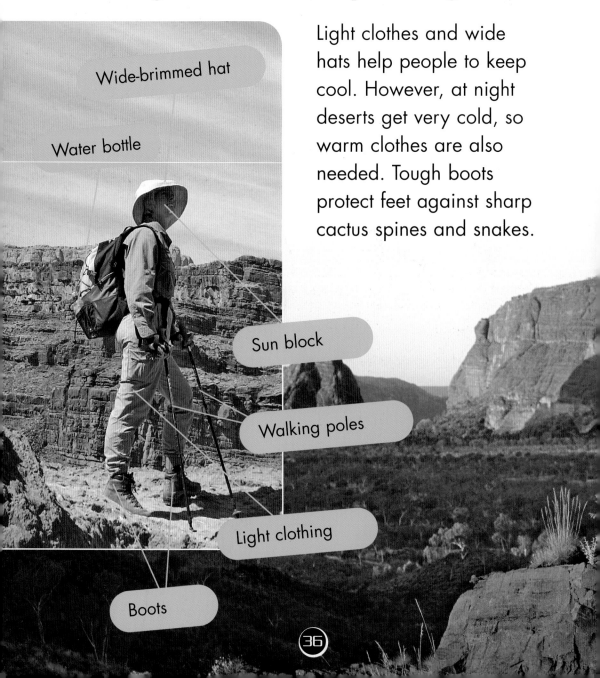

Wide-brimmed hat

Water bottle

Sun block

Walking poles

Light clothing

Boots

It is hard to cross a desert. Huge sand dunes block the way and cars can get stuck in the soft sand. Camels are the perfect desert transport. Why do you think the camel is called the "ship of the desert"?

GT Top Fact

In 1994, Italian runner Mauro Prosperi got lost in the Sahara desert after a sandstorm. He survived by drinking the blood of bats!

ONLINE//:

www.desertusa.com/mag99/mar/stories/desertsur.html
Check out this website for great information on desert survival, including a survival kit, desert animals and desert-linked videos .

At the poles

At the poles it's incredibly cold and windy. Brrrr! The ground is covered in a thick layer of ice. Snow storms, called blizzards, can bury things deep in snow.

This Inuit man is wearing a hooded jacket called a parka.

To survive at the poles it is important to stay warm and dry. If someone gets too cold, they can easily die. Arctic peoples, such as the Inuit, wear thick jackets and boots. Many explorers also wear sun goggles, as looking at the bright snow can make people blind.

An igloo built from ice provides shelter from freezing winds. There are no edible plants in these freezing conditions, so people hunt seals or penguins for food. Near the North Pole, explorers watch out for fierce polar bears.

Go Turbo Survival Skill

Beware of deep cracks in the ice, called crevasses. In 1903, polar explorer Robert Scott fell down one, but managed to climb out.

Igloos have a single entrance to stop heat escaping.

ONLINE//:

www.pbs.org/wnet/nature/fun/arctic_flash.html
Learn how the Inuit people use Arctic animals to help them survive on the ice, plus play the penguin Antarctic survival game.

Rescue

Survivors must let others know where they are if they are to be rescued.

Here are the best ways to let a rescue boat or helicopter know where you are:
- Light a fire in a high place.
- Use a mirror or piece of glass to reflect sunlight.
- Flash a torch on and off.

GT Top Fact

Mountain rescue teams often use dogs to find survivors. They follow **scent** carried on the air, even if people have been buried under an avalanche.

Helicopters are often used to carry out rescues. If the helicopter can't land, it can hover and winch up survivors.

Go Turbo Survival Skill

Many explorers and sailors carry flares with them in case of an emergency. Hand flares (above) can be waved. Flare pistols fire bright flares high into the sky.

ONLINE//:

www.mountain.rescue.org.uk   Find out more about the brave members of the UK Mountain Rescue Service and their skills and equipment. There's also good advice for hillwalkers.

Fast facts

Plants such as bamboo and vines, and some roots, often hold water. The giant Saguaro cactus holds lots of liquid – but it's poisonous.

To avoid stinging insects and spiders, explorers shake clothes and boots before they put them on.

In a desert, people must drink enough water. In the heat an adult needs to drink 10–15 litres of water every day.

When Arctic explorer John Franklin ran out of food in 1822, he tried to eat his leather boots.

In 1992, an avalanche swept Colby Coombs and two friends down a mountain. Over 4 days, Colby struggled back down the mountain. He was the only one to survive.

Poon Lim holds the world record for longest survival adrift at sea. He spent 133 days in a wooden raft after his ship was sunk in 1942. He caught fish and birds to eat and drank their blood.

Answers

These are suggested answers to questions in this book. You may find that you have other answers. Talk about them with your friends. They may have other answers too.

Page 7: The answer to this question will depend on your own opinion.

Page 9: Polar explorers can only take what they can carry and drag on sledges. Important equipment includes very warm clothing, sun goggles and gloves, boots, skis, sledges, ice picks, a snow shovel, rope, a gas stove and pot, a tent, food, maps and a **GPS** device.

Page 17: A=bear, B=deer, C=wolf, D=rabbit. Don't forget, some wild animals such as bears or wolves might be following you!

Page 33: If you meet a bear, put your hands in the air to look bigger, then back away. If you have a backpack, throw it at the bear. It might give you time to escape – but don't run because the bear will chase you.

Pages 35: Camels are called "ships of the desert" because they are the most reliable way of travelling in tough desert conditions. They don't have to drink often, can travel long distances and have wide padded feet so they don't sink into the sand.

Mor website_

A great site with a wide range of information on survival skills and articles written by bushcraft experts:

www.thesurvivalexpert. co.uk

This site has some useful information on what to do in a natural disaster such as a flood, tornado or hurricane:

www.survivaltech niques.net

Everything you want to know about survival expert Bear Grylls:

www.beargrylls.com

Facts about some of the world's most famous explorers:

www.enchantedlearn ing.com/explorers

A wide range of videos on different aspects of bushcraft:

www.azbushcraft.com

Everything you need to know about Scouting in Australia and New Zealand:

**www.scouts.com.au
www.scouts.org.nz**

Test your helicopter rescue skills with this Flash-based mountain rescue game from the BBC:

http://www.bbc.co.uk/ drama/rockface/game/ main.swf

Website of the Central Queensland rescue helicopter, featuring team profiles, a photo gallery and news stories:

www.cqrescue.com.au

Find out more about Gow and Adams's Antarctic expedition (page 9), including a blog and interactive maps, plus Ernest Shackleton's original expedition:

http://shackleton centenary.org

Glossary

Aborigines – the first people who lived in Australia and Tasmania.

Avalanches – a large amount of snow that slides down a mountain.

Bushcraft – the skills needed to survive in the wild, e.g. finding food and making tools.

Compass – a device used for finding your way. Compass needles always point north.

Dehydration – when the body loses too much water, e.g. from sweating.

Fire steel – a rod made of mixed metals that produces sparks when scraped with steel.

Flares – devices for making very bright light to attract help.

Flint – a hard stone struck with a piece of steel to create a spark – perfect for lighting fires.

GPS – global positioning system, a satellite system that allows people to find their position anywhere on Earth.

Leeches – blood-sucking creatures that look like slugs.

Malaria – a disease spread by the bite of a mosquito.

Motto – a word or phrase that sums up the ideals of a group.

Nutrients – the chemicals humans, animals and plants need to grow and stay alive.

Poisonous – something that contains poison and is dangerous to eat.

Rapids – part of a river with rocks and rough water making it dangerous for river craft.

Scent – smell left behind by a person or animal that allows them to be tracked.

Scout – a person who goes ahead to explore, find a route or look out for danger.

SOS – Save Our Souls, world-wide signal for help.

Tinder – dry wood shavings, or other material used to start a fire.

Tipi – a Native American tent made of bison skin stretched over a frame of wooden poles (and shaped like a cone).

Wilderness – a wild place with no or very few people.

Index